BRIAN

Holding the H...

BRIAN MOSES lives in the small Sussex village of
Crowhurst with his wife, two daughters, a loopy
labrador and a collection of bad-tempered chickens.

He first worked as a teacher but has now been a
professional children's poet since 1988. To date he has
over 190 books published and has sold over 1 million
copies of his poetry books and anthologies. Brian also
visits schools to run writing workshops and perform
his own poetry and percussion shows. To date he has
visited well over 2500 schools and libraries throughout
the UK and abroad. He has made several appearances
at the Edinburgh Festival and has been writer in
residence at RAF schools in Cyprus.

Find out more about Brian Moses at
www.brianmoses.co.uk
and at www.nationalpoetryarchive.org

Also by Brian Moses

BRIAN MOSES

Holding the Hands of Angels

Poems from a Seaside Childhood

❖

CHILDREN'S POETRY LIBRARY
No. 13

SALT

LONDON

To Kiera —
Enjoy poems.

PUBLISHED BY SALT PUBLISHING
Acre House, 11–15 William Road, London NW1 3ER,
United Kingdom

First published 2011

Printed in the UK by the MPG Books Group

Typeset in Oneleigh 11 / 14

ISBN 978 1 84471 297 7 paperback

1 3 5 7 9 8 6 4 2

CONTENTS

ACKNOWLEDGEMENTS

'The Wrong Side' first appeared in *Another Third Poetry Book* (Oxford University Press, 1988); "The Bonfire at Barton Point' and 'Climbing the Cemetery Wall' in *Don't Look at Me in That Tone of Voice* (Macmillan, 1998), 'Boys' in *The Teacher's Revenge* (Macmillan, 2003); 'The Family Book' and 'Playing to Win' in *New Angles, Book 2* (Oxford University Press, 1987); 'The Perfect Kiss' in *Snoggers* (Macmillan, 1995); 'Christmas Day' in *A Christmas Stocking* (Cassell, 1988) "The Hate' in *Barking Back at Dogs* (Macmillan, 2000) and 'Billy's Coming Back' in *Taking Out the Tigers* (Macmillan, 2005).

HOLDING THE HANDS OF ANGELS

It's the sort of thing
I look back on now & think, 'Wow,
what was I doing?'
Climbing some cliff face,
risking my life
and for what?

It was dares, of course,
dares and challenges.
Chicken if you didn't,
so we did.
Bet you can't climb to that ledge,
bet you can't reach that cave.

And it was miraculous
that nothing happened.

It wasn't till now
that I realised why.
We must have been
holding the hands
of angels.

All those times
we wriggled back,
a hair breadth from disaster,
cut and scratched,
sticky-plastered,

angels were watching us,
guiding our feet,
pulling us back
from the lightning crack of ice
on a frozen lake.

We believed ourselves invincible,
didn't think how
water drowns,
bones break,
skulls crack....

It's the sort of thing
I look back on now and think, 'Wow,
what was I doing?'

THE WRONG SIDE

My mother used to tell me
I'd got out of bed
on the wrong side, which was strange,
as there was only one side
I could tumble from.

The other was hard against the wall
and all I did was bang
my knee, but still she insisted
that she was right.
So one bright morning
I tried it out, squeezed
between the wall and my bed,
then said nothing.
She never knew. I was puzzled.

My mother said how she'd teach me
to choose between wrong and right,
but if I got out the right side
and that was wrong,
then who was right?

FIRE

There was a fire in our house
when I was a boy,
a living, breathing family fire
that we'd sit in front of,
warming feet or hands
in cold weather.
We'd be blocking the heat
from the rest of the room
till Dad would say, 'Let's feel
the warmth.' Or if we forgot
to close the door he'd yell,
'Were you born in a barn?'
or, 'Put the wood in the hole,
keep the heat in.'
It was true what he said,
heat would leave through
an open door, and even a closed room
would have cold spots,
icy places where you never
felt warm at all.
There were compensations of course
in stories by the fire, figures
in the flames, shadows dancing
on the walls, muffins
held against the embers
till they toasted.

Nothing like that these days.
Coming home, coming in from
the street, to be met
by the warmth from radiators
with a cosy and safe sort of heat
that could never fuel
the imagination.

VACCINATION

When the notes came round
and I read that terrible word,
VACCINATION,
I knew just what to expect.

I'd heard from Ben's brother last year,
how he couldn't move his arm.
He wore it in a sling for weeks,
it went sceptic, where they rammed it in,
came up in a lump — the needle
was huge — like a bicycle pump.

It needed three nurses to hold him down.
He'd been gagged, blindfolded,
while the needle jiggered and jumped around
like a road drill, and all the while he'd howled.

Dad didn't help either —
'In the army,' he said, 'They lined you up —
thump, thump, thump!
When it got to you
the needle was blunt.'

Even navvies and lorry drivers faint,
some nurse said when I once had
a blood test.

But I'd rather suffer all kinds of diseases,
I'd rather meet with blood-sucking leeches.

And the days tick away, one by one,
as ever closer that BIG NEEDLE comes!

WAIT AND SEE....

Dad was a 'wait and see' man.
Decisions took days to arrive.
I knew I'd get nowhere
if I needled and whined.
He'd take his time and then maybe,
when all the heavenly bodies had realigned
and the time was right,
he'd say what he'd decided,
'Yes, you can' or 'No, you can't.'

With some dads, 'wait and see'
meant you'd probably be OK,
get what you wanted, given time.
Not mine. He'd need working on
by Mum. She'd get round him,
make him think it was his idea
all along.

She knew what he'd been like,
he'd been slow to decide all his life —
new house, new carpets, new furniture,
new stereo system — 'Let's sleep on it,'
he'd say, as if in the night
some visitation would appear
and give him a sign, so in the morning
he'd know which decision was right.

Dad was always a 'wait and see' man
and sometimes it seemed an eternity,
all those times I waited and saw
whether what Dad finally decided
was what I was hoping for.

TORTOISE

We didn't know how they were treated then,
bringing them in by the barrel load,
used as little more than a ship's ballast,
lucky if half survived the journey.
We were just pleased to be given one,
male, we thought, and fast for a tortoise.

Each year he steadily ate up Dad's plants
till home from work Dad would yank him out
from between the rows of beans, his snap-jaws
still gripping a tender shoot, mouth stained green.
Then nothing stopped dad from banishing him
to prison in a concrete backyard.

Our dog would rush out and notice him there,
roll him over and abandon him.
He was hopeless, of course, once on his back,
someone would frantically yell, 'Hey quick,
the tortoise, we mustn't leave him like that!'
Guiltily too, we'd be rushing home
from summer days exploring the beach,
he'd be as we feared, legs pedalling air
till once righted again, he'd resume
his interrupted daily attempt to
make it back to dad's vegetable patch.

Someone we knew had a three legged one
that lolloped and limped around the garden
but ours was healthy in every way
seeking gaps in the fence so he might mate
with another walking rock next door!

Then one day he simply just disappeared,
no 'see you soon' and no farewell note,
he eloped with his green-eyed lady love,
dug under two fences and vanished.
We advertised of course, sent messages,
tied a yellow ribbon to the gatepost,
but we should have painted on his shell
an address and number to contact us
if anyone ever noticed him.

These days they'd fit him with a microchip,
have him straight back in no time at all.
But then when he made his one epic trip,
we were tortoiseless, we missed him like mad,
and although he wouldn't admit it,
so did my Dad!

BONNIE AND RONNIE

I wasn't supposed to play
with Bonnie and Ronnie.
It was rumoured they never washed,
they wore tidelines on their necks.

They swore and smoked, picked up butts
and salvaged the good tobacco.
They scooped up dog's muck and threw it,
they were horrible, and they knew it!

You never played tag with Bonnie and Ronnie,
you didn't want them to touch you.
If they did, you washed the place at once
and kept on washing it everyday —
you never knew what might grow there.

There was nothing in their garden.
It looked like those pictures we'd seen
of battlefields after the shelling.
You held your nose as you hurried by,
worried the smell was contagious.

We never saw their dad without a fag
in his mouth or a week's growth of stubble.
A string vest covered his mighty chest.
Coming home he'd call for his

two little terrors, then wrap them
in his huge tatooed arms and squeeze
till they yelled for mercy.

I wasn't supposed to play
with Bonnie and Ronnie,
but I did!

THE BONFIRE AT BARTON POINT

The bonfire at Barton Point
was a wonderful sight, a spectacular blaze,
stuff legends are made of, wicked, ace!
We were talking about it for days.

There were bee hives, signboards, slats and tables,
car tyres, a sledge and a wrecked go-cart,
a radiogram with a case of records,
some put-together furniture that must have pulled
       apart.

And like patients forsaken in mid operation
there were three piece suites in states of distress,
gashes in sides, stuffing pulled out,
and a huge Swiss roll of a mattress.

And we knew we'd need some giant of a guy
to lord it over a pile like this,
not a wimp in a baby's pushchair
that the flames would quickly dismiss.

But on the great and glorious night
we found it hard to believe our eyes
as tilted and tumbled onto the fire
came a whole procession of guys.

Then adults took over and just to ensure
the pile of guys would really burn,
they doused the heap with paraffin
so no ghost of a guy could return.

Then matches flared, torches were lit
at several points around the fire,
till suddenly everything caught at once
and fingers of flame reached higher.

And beaming guys still peered through smoke
till the fiery serpent wrapped them round
in coils of flame, and they toppled down
to merge with the blazing mound.

With our faces scorched, we turned away,
driven back by waves of heat
till after a time the fire slumped back,
its appetite replete.

Now as long as we live we'll remember
Barton Point with its fiery display,
and the charred and blackened treasures
that we pulled from the ashes next day.

LEARNING TO SWIM

Six weeks to learn to swim.
Six weeks and each time our turn came,
it rained or the wind blew,
whipping up waves on the open pool,
strong enough to sink battleships.
No way that I could stay afloat.
I tried my best but my teacher snarled,
'Fingers away from the edge,
I don't want to say it again.'
And if I persisted, his foot
would lay over my hand
like the touch of a butterfly,
till suddenly he'd press down hard
and I'd yell and let go.
And the water would flow
into my mouth and up my nose,
and I'd scream an underwater scream,
then surface, gasp and wheeze,
while all the while it seemed
I'd breathed my last.
He claimed each year that everyone swam
by the time they left his class,
but I beat him....
I didn't.

TALL STORIES

'We've got a pylon at the end of our garden.'

'Oh that's nothing,
we've got a gasometer.'

'Oh yeah, well we've got
a weather research station
that's manned by the Russians.'

'You haven't!'

He hadn't.

So we bashed him!

Graham was always wanting to get one better.
We all knew they were tall stories,
the kind you read in some Sunday papers:
Aliens stole my underpants
or *Baby Nessies discovered in garden pond.*

But he never tired of telling them,
no matter what,
no matter how much we yelled or thrashed him,
he'd come back for more.

Daft really, you'd think he'd have learnt.

Like after the hurricane
with everyone saying:
'A tree blew down in my garden,'
or 'We've lost the roof of our shed.'

Graham had to go and say
he'd half his house missing,
and when we took a look
there were only a couple of slates come down.

I don't know why he did it,
he knew he'd be found out,
told off, walloped.

He knew the story about the boy who cried 'Wolf'
but nothing made any difference.

He'd tell stories about his dad too,
where he worked, what he did.

'My dad's a stuntman,' he'd tell us,
or 'My dad's shooting bears in Alaska.'

but when his dad left home,
Graham didn't say anything.

OUR DITCH

I sat and thought one day
of all the things we'd done
with our ditch; how we'd jumped across
at its tightest point, till I slipped,
came out smelling,
then laid a pole from side to side,
dared each other to slide along it.
We fetched out things that others threw in,
lobbed bricks at tins, played Poohsticks.
We buried stuff in the mud and the gunge
then threatened two girls with a ducking.
We floated boats and bombed them,
tiptoed along when the water was ice
till something began to crack, and we scuttled back.
We borrowed Mum's sieve from the baking draw,
scooped out tadpoles into a jar
then simply forgot to put them back.
(We buried them next to the cat.)
Then one slow day in summer heat
we followed our ditch to where ditch
became stream, to where stream fed river
and river sloped off to the sea.
Strange, we thought, our scrap of water
growing up and leaving home,
roaming the world and lapping
at distant lands.

DRAINS

You can play outside but don't mess about
   near drains, — my mother's advice
as I unlatched the gate and looked for lessons
    the street could teach me.

   The nasty boys up the road looked
into drains, they reached down and fisted out
   pennies. I knew they'd fall prey
    to some terrible plague.

Later I learned to drop bangers down drains,
   held them fused till they almost blew
   then let them fall to the muck below,
hearing the CRUMP of some deep explosion.

   Sometimes tankers came to the street
and workmen lowered hoses, thick as anacondas,
   to slurp and sway till the drains were dry.

   All my nightmares slunk from drains,
   their bulbous heads and shrunken forms
    danced shadows on my walls.

   Mother said there was nothing, no need
for worry at all. She talked away devils

and held back the night, but still my doubts
came crowding back — not everything
my mother said was right.

THE NORTH FACE

This is the famous north face of our teacher
that's never been known to crack a smile.

This is the famous north face of our teacher,
few have scaled the heights to please her.

Some of us have tried and failed,
some of us knew we hadn't a hope,
some of us were brushed aside
or slid back down the slippery slope.

Not for her any creature comforts,
not for her any softening smile,
only the bleak and icy wastes,
of her glacial grimace.

This is the famous north face of our teacher,
all signs of weakness displease her.

But when our headteacher wanders in
and says what lovely work we've done,
there's a glimmer of something
that plays on her lips
like a hint of sun between mountains,
only to vanish again
when she starts to speak.

BOYS

'Now let that be a lesson,' he'd say,
when he gave us three whacks with the slipper.
And for a while it certainly was,
it was brutal medicine
and we weren't too keen to repeat the dose.
The slipper stung and we squeezed eyes tight
to stem any sign of tears.
But memory, like pain, soon wore off
and we'd mess about again.
Like a badge of dishonour
that we pinned on our chests
we counted up how many times
he'd whacked us,
how many times we'd suffered in silence
afraid to let go a yell.
And there wasn't much pleasure
in a school day with him —
number work, scripture, science, composition,
little variation in the daily routine
and nothing we could do to make him smile.
The girls, of course, came off OK
they were never punished at all,
not even if they did the same as us —
talk when they shouldn't, act stupid,
play the fool, he always kept
his temper with them, never lost his cool.

But boys were just an irritation,
to be squashed like insects, their spirits broken.
Nasty, foul-mouthed little creatures
who couldn't behave to save their lives.
So long as he could he would make boys suffer,
it would be his teacher's revenge.

THE HATE

We began each morning with hymns,
'Lots of wind,' our teacher called
as she wrestled a melody
from the ancient hall piano.

Then we sat and gazed at the front
while the football results were read
and Donald was led in, held by the arm,
a look of alarm on his face.
I didn't know what he'd done,
perhaps he'd stolen or two-fingered
once too often. It must have been serious
in the eyes of God, in the eyes
of our headmistress.

She seemed to think
that boys' backsides were meant to be whacked,
but Donald struggled and lay on the floor
and flapped like a fish out of water.
Even the toughies were terrified
as the slipper rose and fell
a total of eighteen times till it stopped
and Donald stayed locked to the floor.

The piano was open but no one played
as we filed out silent and found our maths.
It stayed on our minds for much of the day
but Donald wouldn't say what he'd done
just shook his head and said nothing.

Our teacher said Donald would be forgiven,
start once again and clean the slate.
But I glimpsed him next day in prayers,
a dreadful look on his face, and I knew
it would take more than Jesus
to wipe away the hate.

BILLY'S COMING BACK

There's a sound outside of running feet,
somebody, somewhere's switched on the heat,
policemen are beating a swift retreat
now Billy's coming back.

Only last year when he went away
everyone heaved a sigh,
now news is out, and the neighbourhood
is set to blow sky-high.

Words are heard in the staff room,
teachers' faces deepen with gloom,
can't shrug off this feeling of doom
now Billy's coming back.

It was wonderful when he upped and left,
a carnival feeling straightaway,
no looking over shoulders,
each day was a holiday.

And now like a bomb, no one dares to defuse,
time ticks on while kids quake in their shoes,
no winners here, you can only lose,
now Billy's coming back.

It's dog eat dog on the street tonight,
it's cat and mouse, Billy's looking for a fight,
so take my advice, keep well out of sight
now Billy's coming back.

THE BULLY

The bully was always waiting
down the lane by the big tree
or further along at the churchyard gate.

He was someone to steer clear of,
something to avoid, if you could,
like a bad smell from a blocked drain.

He was dangerous,
like a piranha.
One scowl could strip you to the bone.

Most times he wanted sweets,
some days money.
Money made him smile,
money meant you were all right,
safe, for a while.

Once he twisted my arm
so far behind my back
I thought it would snap.

I closed my eyes and screamed inside.
If you let him know it hurt you
he'd do it all the more.

That was when I had no money to give
and I'd eaten my sweets,
but he must have smelt the chocolate
on my breath.

Then the postman came by
and heard the commotion.

'All right lad,' he said.
'Let him go.'
'That lad's bad,' he said.
I didn't need telling that.

The next time no one saved me.
I shouted and waved my free arm
but it HURT, it hurt like mad,
all day and all the next day too.
There had to be something I could do.

Dad would have said
'Fight your own battles.'
Mum was too busy to notice:
'I broke an arm today Mum.'
'Oh lovely,' she'd say absent-mindedly,
'You must have worked hard.'

Robin Hood wouldn't have stood for it.
He'd have rounded up Little John
and Will Scarlet and let the bully have it.
So I talked to Beryl,
Beryl who helped out on dangerous missions
for a packet of salt and vinegar
or a bag of potato sticks.

She said she could fix him.
It would cost of course,
these things always did.
Hit women come expensive.

When he caught me that night
on the road home,
I knew he'd got it coming.
I almost told him.

Next morning Beryl tipped him up
in the mud at the side of the road.
She, and the flying squad she controlled,
ran to school with his trousers.

In the playground, we wound down
the Union Jack that flapped
at the top of our flag pole,
then tied his trousers to the wire
and raised them as high as we could.

When the bully appeared he was crying,
he was actually crying,
and for one brief awful moment
I almost felt sorry for him.

We wound down his trousers
and handed them back.
He didn't say anything,
just wiped his face
with the flat of his hand
and took them away.

Later that day he found me
in a spot just short of home.
He stood at some distance
and scowled. 'I'll get you,'
he spat. 'I'll make you pay,
if it takes all year,
if it takes….'

'And we'll get you too,'
I blurted out.
'We'll pay you back
in a different way.'

He spat again,
just missing my feet,
then turned and stomped off
down our street.

WHEN BILLY CAME BACK...

Nobody felt safe anymore,
the bully was out to settle old scores.
Everyone vanished behind closed doors...

When Billy came back...
when Billy came back...

He was solid, built like a lumberjack,
It was permanent alert, he was out to attack,
no colours anymore, everything looked black...

When Billy came back...
when Billy came back...

And Billy wasn't happy till he'd made someone cry,
he'd twist your ear and jab at your eye,
then sneeringly say, 'You're about to die.'

When Billy came back...
when Billy came back...

Like a heat seeking missile, he'd home in on you,
a volcanic explosion as his anger grew,
you'd be begging for mercy by the time he was
        through...

When Billy came back…
when Billy came back…

And everyone else would be urging him on
saying, 'Go on Billy, give him one for me.'
For when Billy was beating up somebody else,
then Billy was leaving you be.

When Billy came back…
when Billy came back…

And it wasn't just bottles, it was bones he
           smashed…

When Billy came back…
when Billy came back…
when Billy came back…

THE COWPAT THROWING CONTEST

Malc and me and Ian Grey, we couldn't believe
when we heard someone say, that in cattle towns
of the old Wild West, they held cowpat throwing
       contests!

How awful, how dreadful, what if it hit
you smack in the mouth, you'd gag, you'd be sick,
but we knew, even then, the day would come when we'd
       try it.

And it wasn't very long after that when the three of us
were sent away — 'Get out of the house,
get out of my sight, go somewhere else and play.'

And we walked until the houses stopped, looked
over a hedge and there in a field were pancakes of
the very stuff we'd been talking about for days.

The cows looked friendly so we started up
with a chunk or two that might have been mud
but we knew we'd move on to the slimy stuff before
       long.

Malc was the first to try it out and scooped up
a really terrible lump, but while Ian was yelling
and backing away, he tripped and sat down in the dung.

Malc was laughing fit to burst and he must have
        forgotten
his hands were full till he dropped the lot
all down his trousers, then wiped his hands on his shirt.

I made the mistake of grinning too till Malc hit my
        jacket
and Ian my shoes, and I watched it spreading
        everywhere,
while the cows just stood there and mooed!

Well, after that it was in our hair and down our
        jumpers
and everywhere. Our fingernails were full of the stuff,
then Ian said, 'Pax, I've had enough.'

'We look awful,' Malc said, 'And we smell as sweet as
a sewage farm in the midday heat. We shouldn't have
        done it,
we've been really daft' — but Ian just started to laugh.

We laughed up the lane while a cloud of flies
trailed us back to Ian's place, where his mum's grim
        face
soon shut us up as she fixed her hose to the tap.

'It's history, Mum, it's really true. It's what they did
in the Wild West — ' but we lost the rest of what he
        said
as a jet of water pounded his chest.

Then water was turned on Malc and me, and we both
        went home
in Ian's clothes, while his mum phoned ours and tried
to explain just what it was that we'd done.

I knew my mum would have a fit. 'That's it,'
she said, 'the final straw. No way you're going out
to play for a week, no, a month, maybe more.'

'Get in that bath, use plenty of soap, how could you be
such a silly dope? Use the nailbrush too and wash
your hair. I'll be in there later to check.'

I scrubbed and I brushed but I couldn't make the smell
disappear, and I wondered how the cowboys coped
when their contest was done and everyone climbed in
        the tub.

And kids held their noses and called out, 'Pooh!'
for days and weeks and months after that, but it didn't
        matter,

we'd proved we were best, not at spellings or sport
or school reports, but at cowpat throwing contests.

CHRISTMAS DAY

It was waking early and making a din.
It was knowing that for the next twenty minutes
  I'd never be quite so excited again.
It was singing the last verse of
  'O Come all Ye Faithful', the one that's
  only meant to be sung on Christmas Day.
It was lighting a fire in the unused room
  and a draught that blew back woodsmoke
  into our faces.
It was lunch and a full table,
  and dad repeating how he'd once eaten his
  off the bonnet of a lorry in Austria.
It was keeping quiet for the Queen
  and Gran telling that one about children
  being seen but not heard.
  (As if we could get a word in edgeways
  once she started!)
It was 'Monopoly' and me out to cheat the Devil
  to be the first to reach Mayfair.
It was, 'Just a small one for the lad,'
  and dad saying, 'We don't want him getting tiddly.'
It was aunts assaulting the black piano
  and me keeping clear of mistletoe
  in case they trapped me.
It was pinning a tail on the donkey,

and nuts that wouldn't crack
and crackers that pulled apart but didn't bang.

And then when the day was almost gone,
  it was Dad on the stairs,
  on his way to bed,
  and one of us saying:
    'You've forgotten to take your hat off....'
  And the purple or pink or orange paper
  still crowning his head.

'tiddly' — my Dad's word to describe someone who
drank a bit more alcohol than he should have done.

SLEDGING

Somewhere in the shed, buried under tools,
sacks, stacks of wood, there's a sledge,
knocked together years ago, in days when
snow was snow, till now that is.
Now five inches have fallen overnight,
school shut down, the day stretched ahead.
A real reason now to spring out of bed,
'Snow, it's snow, I didn't know,
I just don't remember what it was like.'
I won't have breakfast, grab some toast,
kick into my boots and zip up my coat,
pull out my sledge from the shed.
Then hike up the hill out back of my house,
lie flat down and let myself go,
skimming down fast over powdery snow.
It's one huge thrill on Breakneck Hill,
our very own Cresta run, with the snow
packed down, trodden in, mirror smooth.
I hope it will last and not disappear
as fast as it came. Our winters
will never be the same, now that we know
what snow is like. And there's time to slide
again and again, climb back to
the top, lie down and then go
over snow, over snow, over wonderful snow.

THE FAMILY BOOK

My father unlocks the family book
where the captured Victorians sit
tight-lipped, keeping their own closed counsel.
I find them caught at christenings
as the 'greats' collect with the 'latest'
and another name is tied to the family line;
or posed (but not poised) in studios,
the fathers and sons from their Sunday slumbers,
suited and sober and seemingly shy
as if their souls could be stolen away
for the price of a print on paper.

I watch my father separate the 'great greats'
from the 'great', the proud patriarchs,
the weddings and unsmiling aunts,
the fishermen released from their nets,
the light keeper and his shiny wife.
I flick back the pages and try to find
my fingerprints in their faces.

FISHING SUMMER

Michael and I were fishing companions
rushing to catch the tide before it turned,
our tackle spilling from saddlebags, our
pockets crammed with fat paper wallets of
fresh dug lug. And casting we'd encounter
familiar hazards, reels span at our first
attempts, lines tangled, sprouted birds' nests;
we spent precious time unravelling till
tides turned and the fish bit fast. We caught an
old lag of a crab that came up fighting:
It bubbled and spat with vicious claws splayed
out like a baseball catcher, then edged off
sideways across the pier to drop-plop down
to water beneath. There were rumours too
of dreadful beasts that slithered from clefts
in search of food, of monster congers that
wrapped their tails round rocks and then gave battle.
There were times when we wished the big fish would
bite, though we doubted the strength of our tackle.
We'd picture ourselves with fantastic catches,
our photos in angling magazines, but
nothing that size ever gobbled our lines.

Michael and I were fishing companions
packing away with the light slipping by,
before cycling back through dreary streets
while darkness spread its nets all over town.

DAD THREW SNAILS

Dad threw snails out into the street,
hearing the crack of shells
as they smacked against tarmac.
His reasoning was simple:
He grew plants, snails ate them,
so snails should be removed from plants.
It was sporting too, he gave them
a chance, if their shells didn't smash
on impact, or tyres squash them flat,
some, just one or two, crawled back
to be turned up and jettisoned
once again when Dad like an ace
detective uncovered their tracks.
I wondered how he reconciled
his love for all God's gifts with this,
his daily slaughter. Perhaps he imagined
the snail with its horns was something
the Devil had engineered one storm-
tossed night when God's back was turned.
It was one of those troubles sent
to try him, worse of course with rain.
Dad threw snails out into the street
where surprised passers-by found spread
at their feet, a pattern of dazed
and damaged creatures, grey and alien.

HEAVEN

From the top of Breakneck Hill
we thought we might see Heaven,
some space between clouds where light pours through,
the place where the chosen ones would go.

We didn't know, of course, what Heaven looked like:
There were no tourist guides
and no one who went there
came back to tell.

Most of us hoped it would be an endless funfair,
a sweet store where you'd help yourself
again and again,
a Saturday treat or the sort of holiday
that would last forever.

Even the clever ones at school
had no more idea of what Heaven might be
although Sam, who lived for numbers,
said that in all probability it would be
an endless maths lesson.

We pitied him, and thought that such a geeky
        response
didn't warrant any reply.

So we watched the clouds playing tag
across an arc of sky,
then set off home.

Heaven could wait...
There was Doctor Who on TV soon,
Wouldn't that be Heaven enough
for one afternoon?

CLIMBING THE CEMETERY WALL

Jake and me, we're experts at climbing
over the cemetery wall.
We do it almost every day
when we steam our way home from school.
It cuts quite a lot off the journey,
I bunk him or he bunks me,
and we hope the groundsman doesn't see
as we're climbing the cemetery wall.

There's a gap where bricks have fallen
and smashed, there's a ledge
where we stand and grip with our hands
then pull ourselves up by our nails.
But it's not an easy wall to scale
when we're loaded down with homework books,
lunchbox and games gear slung over
our backs as we tackle the difficult climb.

I've missed my footing lots of times,
grazed both knees, torn holes in clothes,
stained my blazer and scuffed new shoes
while climbing the cemetery wall.

But all in all it's for the best
it gets us home before anyone else,
though sometimes, if we're late coming out,
there's a lip-curling, fist whirling
gang of lads whose idea of fun is
fox and hounds, baying like mad
as they hunt us down
while we head for the cemetery wall.

And we haul our bags over the wall
then scramble up as best we can,
but the wall's quite high
and I kneel on my tie, half-strangle myself till I'm
        hoisted up
to lie on the top and catch my breath,
or dangle my legs on the other side,
preparing myself for the drop.

I don't suppose the residents mind,
they're pretty quiet much of the time,
though perhaps one or two, when they were alive,
tried climbing the cemetery wall!

PLAYING TO WIN

Along the length of the town's esplanade,
the arcades rolled up their shutters, prepared
for the summer trade, while necklaced with keys
like strange mayoral chains, attendants
fiddled, filled the machines and waited
for punters like me.

Pintables held no interest, nothing to win,
Instead I'd try for the cherries in rows,
a jackpot of jaffas or prize awards,
my bag in place for the tumbling hordes of
pennies that never came. Or happy on
handles of cranes I'd watch the scoop
while down it dug till the snap-jaws gripped,
then whipped back quickly a cascade of sweets,
stale, uneatable, ammo to fire at
the necks of prowling attendants.

Then later I tried to beat the machines
with buttons or wire or bent foreign coins
till expert at fiddling rolla pennies
I'd leant across to receive my reward
when a hand clamped my shoulder that no amount
of turning or twisting could shift.
Then too frightened to give a false name and
address, I stammered out my lame excuse

while the manager juggled his phone, warned
if he ever caught me again he'd call
the police or my home; and abject I moved
from foot to foot till his hand on my neck
steered me over the floor, where watched by my mates
and held at length, I was booted out through the door.

MISSILES IN CUBA

(In October 1962 America realised that Russian missile launching sites were being built on the Communist island of Cuba, only 90 miles from the coast of America. President Kennedy sent warnings to Khruschev, the Russian president, that this would not be allowed. America then set up a naval blockade or 'quarantine' area around Cuba to prevent the sites from being completed. This brought the two super powers to the brink of nuclear war and for six days the world held its breath . . .)

I was twelve years old
when Kennedy muscled up to Khruschev
over missiles in Cuba,
when Cold War bluff and counter-bluff
took the world to the brink.
I learnt a new word —
Armaggedon —
'It could happen here,'
the papers proclaimed,
'It could happen now.'

I questioned my parents constantly,
were we all about to die?
My father, grim faced,
spoke only of the last lot,
of how they survived.

But the world had rolled on since then,
more fuses, more firepower.
My eyes pleaded with him,
say it will be OK.
But he was frightened too,
I could tell.

We tiptoed about the house,
it didn't seem right to play Elvis songs,
no 'Good Luck Charm' would stop this war,
I knew the score on that one.
And why should I worry about tests at school,
we could all be blown to pieces
come the weekend.

My father said it was prayer that was needed,
but prayer wasn't doing any good.
And I remember that last chance Sunday,
all of us praying in church,
praying so hard it hurt,
then coming home to find
they'd backed away,
stepped down from
the abyss.

Out in the garden
I stood beneath the stars,
breathed in,
breathed deep,
breathed a future

ABOVE THE PIT

From my childhood room I stared at the street,
lit by the glow of a werewolf moon,
past the lorry yard to the mission hall
where tall gates were tightly shut.
Beyond, I knew, were graves in the grass,
a garden of rest that no one tended,
padlocked to keep the curious out
or sinister somethings within.

Now rough feet tramp over ground
no longer sacred. The graves are gone,
shuffled and stacked like cards
then cleared away. They levelled the land
then sank foundations, firm enough
to stand new houses.

And I wondered how deep they'd dug,
remembered what I'd read
of men who moled the London Tube
and how their spades uncovered bones,
the final homes of those who went
plague naked to the burial place.

I was certain no good would come
from building houses in a graveyard.
Already the ground was spread with cracks,

driest summer for twenty years,
but it seemed to me like a scene being set
where everyone's watching TV and then . . .

The carpet buckles, bursts apart,
an arm reaches up
from the pit . . . .

THE GROUP

There wasn't much to do today
so Malcolm and me and Ian Grey
planned how we might form a group
with me on keyboards, Malcolm on drums
and Ian who knew how to strum a C
or a G on his brother's guitar.

Then Ian's sister came waltzing in
with her friend Sharon & wanted to know
why they couldn't be in the group as well
and when we said no, they threatened to tell
some dreadful secret & Ian turned white,
said they could stay if they kept really quiet.

Then we argued a bit about the name:
'The Werewolves' I said or 'The Sewer Rats'
or 'The Anti Everything Parents Say'
but Malc said no, it ought to be simple
and Ian said maybe 'The group with no name'
while his sister and Sharon said something silly
and Malcolm and I ignored them completely

And I thought we ought to write some songs,
'Easy,' we said, 'it wouldn't take long
to knock off another "Hold onto your love,
don't let her go, oh no, no, no!"'

And Malc kept the beat with slaps on his knee
while I played kazoo or a paper and comb
till Sharon yawned, then got up and went home.

Then Ian's sister and Ian sat down
while we stood around and said what to write,
and it sounded all right till we tried it out
and discovered how awful it was
'Let's knock it on the head,' I said,
'We'll need another year or two
before we get it right.'

And later that night on the short walk home
I said to Malc that I thought we ought
to dump the others and go it alone.
We should have seen it all along,
two good looking dudes like us,
we'd be famous in no time.
But Malc said we were overlooking
one small but very important thing:
Neither of us could sing!

BEAN PICKING

Bean picking, one summer with Mike
and two girls I hardly knew.

It was back breaking work
for little cash, but simple.
Even I couldn't make a hash of it.

And Mike was a smooth talker
who rolled from the cradle
bright side up.

He spent most of his time impressing
the girls. I envied his line
in patter, his quick delivery.

I liked to think I might learn
his technique.

And then when it rained we played around
with the girls on the hay in the barn.
All innocent stuff really,
jumping off bales in daredevil stunts.

Till suddenly the playing stopped
and Mike and Brenda paired off,
while Sally was left with me.

I took her hand and we stumbled along
the rows of beans in the rain,
and somewhere in my chest,
in my big kid heart, I felt
the rumblings of first love.

DAD'S GREATCOAT

It was the summer of 1967
when I stole Dad's army greatcoat,
opened the window and dropped it down
to Juliet in the street below.
It was fashionable then, but far too hot
and I melted but wouldn't take it off.
We must have thought we were really hip
with my flared yellow pants from Carnaby Street
and Juliet's kaftan, beads and a flower.
But after an hour it got too much,
I shrugged off the coat and bundled it up,
ran down to the beach and flopped in the sand,
held Juliet's hand for half an hour
but got no further — she wasn't the sort.
She'd give me a peck at her gate later on,
boring really, nothing more, but she'd give me
the most adorable smiles and she told me once
I had style, I had charm, and in
the summer of '67, just being there,
sharing a coke, telling a joke, making her laugh
was heaven enough for me.
(And she even helped me return the greatcoat
surreptitiously . . . .)

MY LIFE IS OVER

My life is over tonight for sure
now that Brenda Barnes has sussed me out,
she'll be telling everyone, no doubt,
how I'm really useless at kissing.

Brenda will broadcast it all round school
so I might as well write my farewell note,
join the Foreign Legion, stowaway on a boat,
now I'm labelled useless at kissing.

I practised in front of the mirror for hours,
puckering up and closing my eyes,
but as from tomorrow I'll be in disguise
when the girls know I'm useless at kissing.

Her lips were like fire, I thought I'd been burned,
I jumped back quickly, she obviously thought
I'd spurned her advances, now my chances are
      nought,
someone please help me practise my kissing.

I know that I shouldn't contemplate this
but there's no way out, my senses are numb,
overnight, please someone, strike Brenda dumb
and keep secret that traumatic kiss.

THE PERFECT KISS

She said:
'Let's try to break the record
for long distance kissing.'

I must have looked askance
till she said:
'Well your mouth's fallen open,
so we might as well start . . .'

And she clamped her lips on mine.

I told her, when we surfaced for air,
that I really liked kissing her.
She tasted of wine and honey,
of some Caribbean brand of toothpaste
that you don't buy at Boots.

She said she imagined
she'd been kissing the leading hunk
in some L.A. detective series on TV;
and she hoped I didn't mind.

But when I got home that night
and slipped some cream on
sore and swollen lips,

I took a look
in the Guinness book —
17 days, 10 hours
in Chicago, U.S.A.

And I thought things like, 'WOW!'

And then how hard
we'd have to practise
to stand any chance
of beating that...

And I wondered what they did,
how they ate, drank,
got by without talking.

Did they kiss in their sleep
and were their lips
ever quite the same again?

Did they spend their lives,
eyes half-closed,,
lips puckered up,
incomplete without the other?

And would they have any tips —
an exercise programme for lips maybe —
to recommend to beginners like me
in seach of the perfect kiss.

THE BOY SCARER

Most of us called her the boy scarer,
timed to make untimely bursts
at five minute intervals.
Like one of those guns that fire all day
to frighten birds from the fields,
she'd say the most horrendous things
and scare the boys away,

'Every time she yacks it's like a smack in the mouth,'
they'd say. 'She's weird, your friend,
she's really crazy.'

It got so bad that we wouldn't walk
down the street with her anymore.
She'd make the daftest remarks
and no one would laugh.

Time flew when she wasn't around,
time dragged when she started sounding off
on things she knew nothing about.

'Every time she opens her mouth
she puts her foot in it.'
Though in her case, both feet,
up to the knees. Perhaps she'll choke,
some hope!

She's a boy scarer,
and like that infernal machine in the fields,
the racket just won't go away.

BENEATH THE STARS

'I will if you will,'
she said.

The sea looked inviting,
the evening had been
exciting.

I didn't know what to do or say,
I didn't want to lose face.

But I couldn't go back
and I heard her call —
'Race you down to the sea,'
as I shuffled along behind.

And turning round we saw lights
from the town, heard the sound
of distant cars,

while we skinnydipped
beneath the stars.

It was lovely!